is it red?
is it yellow?
is it blue?

an adventure
in color by
tana hoban

greenwillow books
An Imprint of HarperCollinsPublishers

Is it Red? Is it Yellow? Is it Blue?
Copyright © 1978 by Tana Hoban
Printed in Hong Kong.
All rights reserved.
www.harperchildrens.com

Library of Congress
Cataloging in Publication Data
Hoban, Tana.
Is it red?
Is it yellow?
Is it blue?
"Greenwillow Books."
Summary: Illustrations and brief
text introduce colors and the
concepts of shape, quantity,
and direction.
ISBN 0-688-80171-4
ISBN 0-688-84171-6 (lib. bdg.)
ISBN 0-688-07034-5 (pbk.)
1. Colors—Juvenile literature.
2. Form perception—Juvenile
literature.   3. Space perception—
Juvenile literature.   (1. Colors.
2. Size and shape.   3. Space
perception.   4. Visual perception.)
I. Title.
BF311.H56   153.7'5   78-2549

15 14

to Jeffrey
and to David, Jeremy and Erica

is it red? is it yellow? is it blue?
an adventure in color

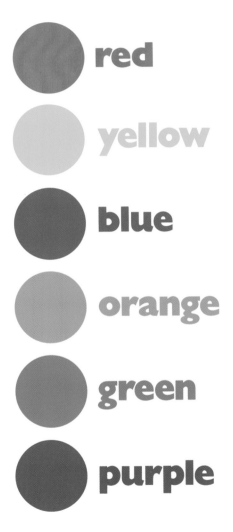

red

yellow

blue

orange

green

purple

Tana Hoban's photographs have been exhibited at the Museum of Modern Art. She has won many gold medals and prizes for her work as a photographer and filmmaker. And, of course, her books for children are known and loved throughout the world. These books include:

SHAPES AND THINGS

LOOK AGAIN!
1971 ALA Notable

COUNT AND SEE
1972 ALA Notable

PUSH·PULL, EMPTY·FULL

OVER, UNDER & THROUGH

WHERE IS IT?

CIRCLES, TRIANGLES AND SQUARES

DIG·DRILL, DUMP·FILL

BIG ONES, LITTLE ONES